I didn't know that **some bugs glow in the dark**

© Aladdin Books Ltd 1997

Produced by

Aladdin Books Ltd

28 Percy Street

London W1P 0LD

First published in the United States in 1997 by

Copper Beech Books,

an imprint of

The Millbrook Press

2 Old New Milford Road

Brookfield, Connecticut 06804

Concept, editorial, and design by

David West Children's Books

Designer: Robert Perry

Illustrators: Myke Taylor, Rob Shone, and Jo Moore

Printed in Belgium

Library of Congress Cataloging-in-Publication Data

Llewellyn, Claire.
Some bugs glow in the dark and other amazing facts about insects / by Claire
Llewellyn ; illustrated by Myke Taylor, Rob Shone, and Jo Moore.
p. cm. — (I didn't know that—)
Includes index.
Summary: Provides information about various insects and their physical
characteristics, homes, feeding habits, and defenses.
ISBN 0-7613-0562-9 (lib. bdg.). — ISBN 0-7613-0587-4 (trade hc)
1. Insects—Miscellanea—Juvenile literature. [1. Insects.] I. Taylor, Myke, ill.
II. Shone, Rob, ill. III. Moore, Jo, ill. IV. Title. V. Series.
QL467.2.L58 1997   96-43331
595.7—dc20   CIP AC

I didn't know that

some bugs glow in the dark

Claire Llewellyn

COPPER BEECH BOOKS
BROOKFIELD, CONNECTICUT

I didn't know that

Introduction

Did *you* know that you would need to use dynamite to blow up a termite's home?

... that stick insects can grow as long as a cat?

... that some wasps lay their eggs in pots?

Discover for yourself amazing facts about the insect world, from the tiniest fairy fly and the high-jumping flea to the insect that eats birds...

Watch for this symbol that means there is a fun project for you to try.

Is it true or is it false? Watch for this symbol and try to answer the question before reading on for the answer.

Don't forget to check the borders for extra amazing facts.

I didn't know that

insects have six legs. *Beetles,* ants and all other insects have three pairs of legs. Counting the legs is a sure way of identifying an insect. Wood lice, spiders, mites, and centipedes aren't insects – they have far too many legs.

Goliath beetle

An insect has three different parts to its body: the head, the *thorax,* and the *abdomen.* A hard outer skeleton makes the insect waterproof and protects its soft insides.

Eye   Brain   Thorax   Stomach

Abdomen

Mouth   Heart   Leg

Woodlouse

The first insects lived 370 million years ago - long before the dinosaurs.

People who study insects are called entomologists. They learn about insects, how and where they live and how best to protect them.

SEARCH & FIND

FIND & SEARCH & FIND

Find one insect and three imposters.

Centipede

Bird-eating spider

There are well over a million kinds of insects in the world. That's more than all the other kinds of animals put together! Entomologists discover 8,000 new insects every year.

7

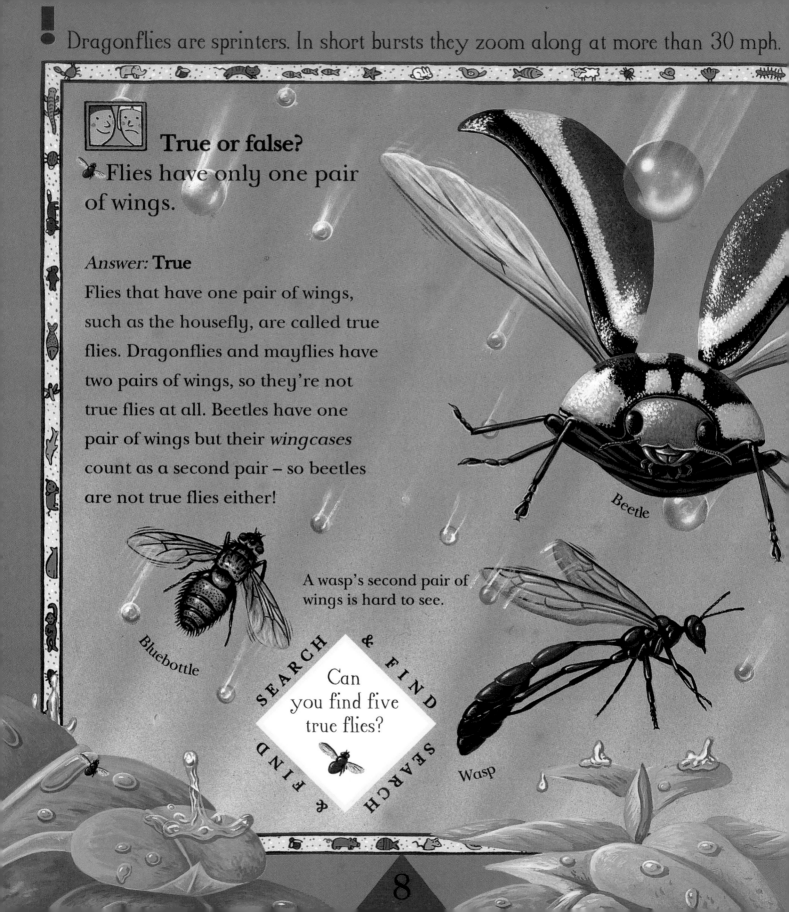

True or false?

🦟 Flies have only one pair of wings.

Answer: **True**

Flies that have one pair of wings, such as the housefly, are called true flies. Dragonflies and mayflies have two pairs of wings, so they're not true flies at all. Beetles have one pair of wings but their *wingcases* count as a second pair – so beetles are not true flies either!

Beetle

A wasp's second pair of wings is hard to see.

Bluebottle

SEARCH & FIND & SEARCH & FIND

Can you find five true flies?

Wasp

8

I didn't know that

beetles can fly. Ladybugs and many other beetles can all fly when they need to. They open up the wingcases on their back, unfold their soft wings, and take off!

Butterfly

Dragonfly

Flying insects survive tropical storms because the raindrops make a breeze as they fall, which blows tiny insects aside. They end up flying between the drops.

A butterfly's wings are covered with rows of scales, arranged like the tiles on a roof. Each scale is like a tiny speck of dust.

Some flies wings can beat 1,000 times a second – that's why flies buzz.

I didn't know that

caterpillars are baby butterflies. Like many insects, butterflies change completely as they grow – from an egg, to a caterpillar, to a *pupa*, to a butterfly. This way of growing is called *metamorphosis*.

The author Franz Kafka wrote a book called Metamorphosis. It's about a man who changed into a giant insect.

SEARCH & FIND

Can you find nine caterpillars?

FIND & SEARCH

10

Not all insects change as they grow. Baby shield bugs look like their parents when they hatch. They just get bigger and bigger, and eventually grow their wings.

Mayflies spend most of their lives as wingless *larvae*. Once they change into adult mayflies, they live for only a day.

! Some caterpillars change into moths, not butterflies.

I didn't know that

some bugs can walk on water. Pond skaters are so light that they can skim across ponds without falling into the water. Hairy tufts on their tiny feet help them to stay afloat.

SEARCH & FIND
Can you find the water snail?
FIND SEARCH &

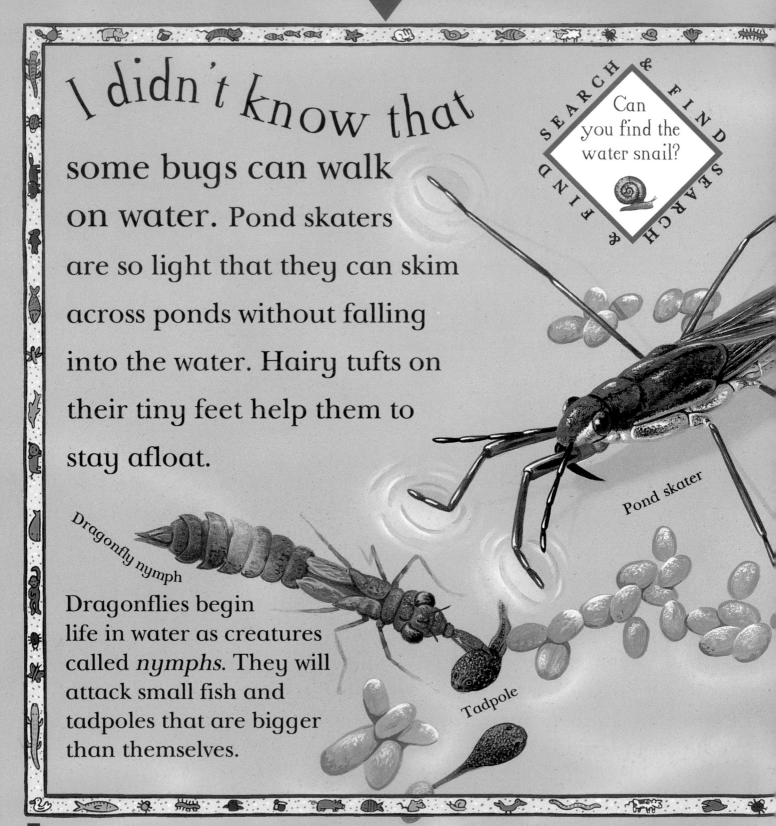

Pond skater

Dragonfly nymph

Dragonflies begin life in water as creatures called *nymphs*. They will attack small fish and tadpoles that are bigger than themselves.

Tadpole

A water boatman lies on his back and rows through the water.

True or false?
Water beetles in lakes and
ponds can breathe under the
water.

Water beetle

Answer: **False**
Water beetles can't breathe under
water. They swim to the surface
to collect air bubbles. These
supply the beetles with air
when they dive
underwater.

The ancient Greeks and
Romans believed that
beautiful nature
goddesses lived in rivers
and streams. They were
called water nymphs.

Tropical weaver ants build their homes out of leaves. Some of the ants hold the leaves together, while others stick them with a sticky glue. The glue comes from larvae the ants carry in their jaws.

I didn't know that

termite mounds have air-conditioning. Termites build themselves tall mud towers, where millions of the insects live. Every tower has a chimney that draws up warm air and keeps the nest cool.

FIND & SEARCH

Can you find the queen termite?

SEARCH & FIND

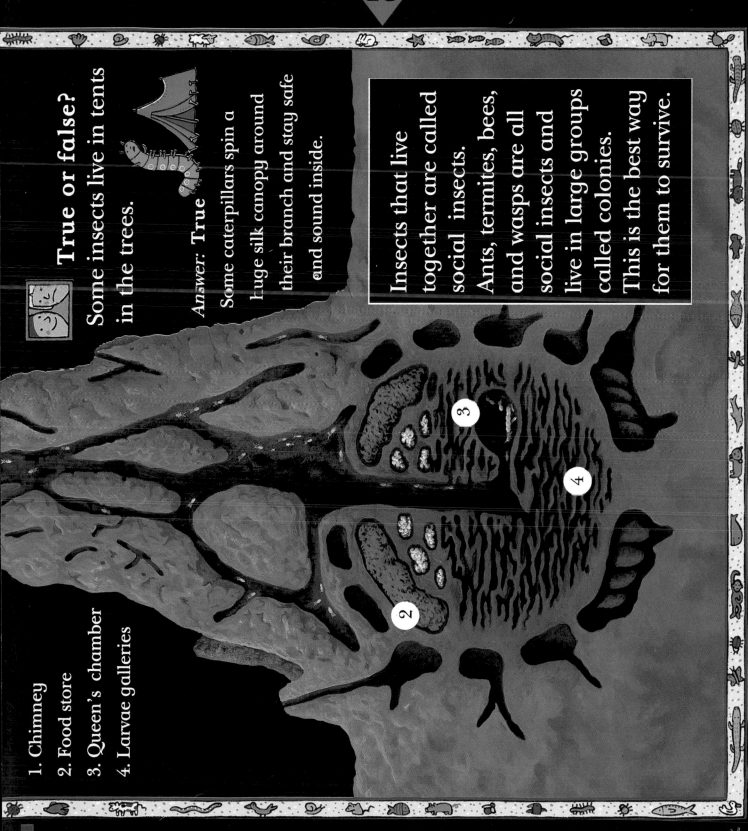

True or false?

Some insects live in tents in the trees.

Answer: **True**

Some caterpillars spin a huge silk canopy around their branch and stay safe and sound inside.

Insects that live together are called social insects.
Ants, termites, bees, and wasps are all social insects and live in large groups called colonies.
This is the best way for them to survive.

1. Chimney
2. Food store
3. Queen's chamber
4. Larvae galleries

Termites make a natural cement by mixing sand with their droppings.

Potter wasp

I didn't know that some wasps build pots. The female potter wasp makes tiny mud pots, and lays an egg in each one. Before sealing a pot, she pokes a *grub* inside – a tasty meal for her young when it hatches.

In ancient Egypt, the dung beetle was the symbol for the sun god, who rolled the sun across the sky each day.

Dung beetle brooch from Ancient Egypt

Most insects don't make nests. They just lay their eggs near some food.

True or false?

Insects make bad parents. They never look after their young.

Answer: **False**

The female fungus beetle cleans and protects her eggs until they hatch. Then she helps the larvae to feed for about two weeks.

Fungus beetle

Dung beetles lay their eggs inside balls of dung – their larvae's favorite food. The beetles make the balls by rolling bits of dung along the ground.

 You can make a giant potter wasp's pot. Roll damp clay into thin ropes, and coil them in circles to make a jar. Copy the shape from the picture (above left). Be sure to make a lip around the top. Smooth the sides and leave it to dry.

True or false?
A honeybee tastes its food with its feet.

Answer: **True**
A honeybee tastes with its feet as well as its mouth. It can sample its food as soon as it lands on it. (So can houseflies.)

Proboscis

Butterflies suck up the *nectar* from flowers through a long tongue called a proboscis. When they're not feeding, they keep it curled up out of the way.

Cockroaches eat anything; meat, bread, fruit, cardboard ....

I didn't know that

ants are great farmers. Just as farmers keep cows, so some kinds of ants keep *aphids*. They protect them from their enemies, and in return the ants "milk" the aphids for the honeydew they suck up.

If you want to study moths you can attract them by leaving a mixture of sugar and water near a lighted, open window at night.

SEARCH & FIND

Can you find the bumblebee?

FIND & SEARCH

19

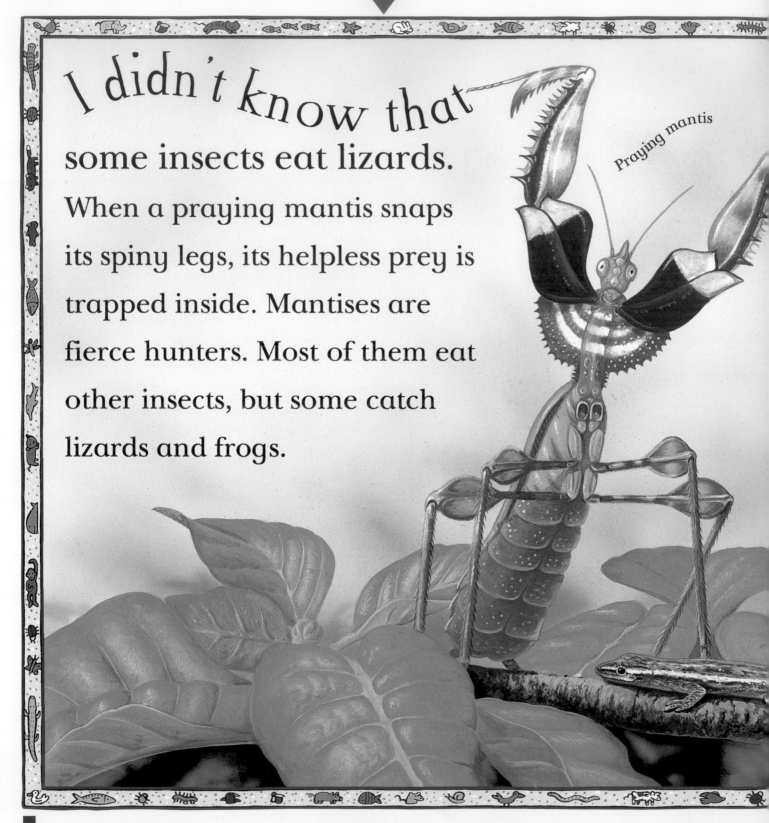

I didn't know that

some insects eat lizards. When a praying mantis snaps its spiny legs, its helpless prey is trapped inside. Mantises are fierce hunters. Most of them eat other insects, but some catch lizards and frogs.

Praying mantis

A female mantis is so dangerous, she'll even eat her mate.

SEARCH & FIND
Can you find the praying mantis' meal?
FIND & SEARCH

Some tropical moths feed on the salty tears of horses and deer. The moths flutter around the animals' eyes to make them cry!

Mosquito

When the assassin bug catches a tasty meal, it injects it with poison. This turns the prey's body to soup. Then the bug sucks it all up.

Not all mosquitoes suck blood – only the females do. They need blood to make their eggs. Male mosquitoes feed on nectar.

Assassin bug

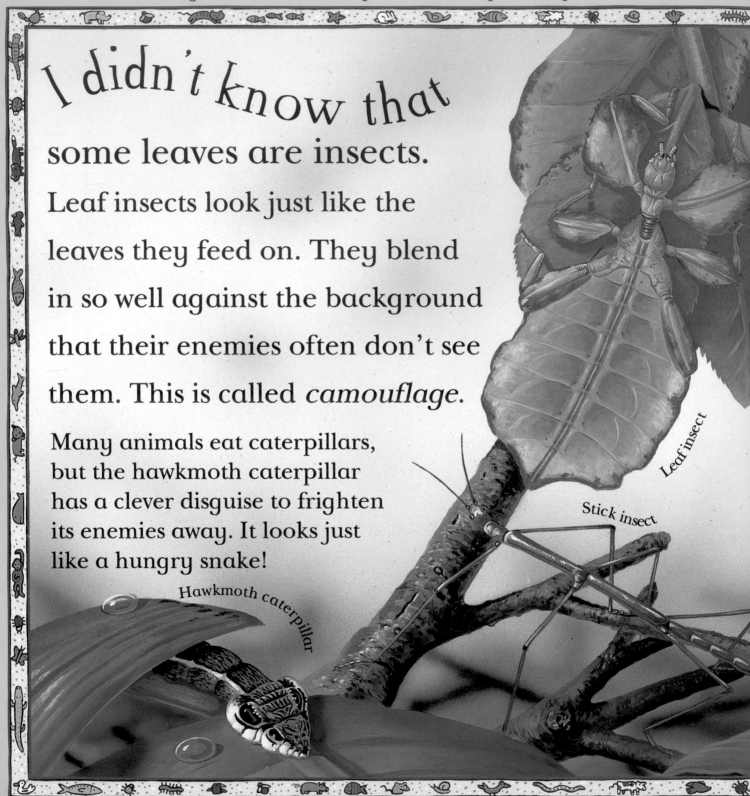

I didn't know that

some leaves are insects. Leaf insects look just like the leaves they feed on. They blend in so well against the background that their enemies often don't see them. This is called *camouflage*.

Many animals eat caterpillars, but the hawkmoth caterpillar has a clever disguise to frighten its enemies away. It looks just like a hungry snake!

Leaf insect

Stick insect

Hawkmoth caterpillar

These fly orchids aren't insects at all but plants that mimic insects. They look like female insects. This attracts the male insects to them that can then pollinate (fertilize) them.

Camouflage isn't only for defense. The pink flower mantis is cleverly hidden inside an orchid – the better to ambush its prey.

Flower mantis

When thorn bugs land on twigs, they look like nasty prickles. And even if they're caught, they're much too sharp to eat.

Thorn bugs

! Many insects are green so they match the leaves they feed on.

I didn't know that

some insects stink.

Stinkbugs are the skunks of the insect world. When they're frightened, they let out a dreadful smell from tiny holes between their legs. This gets rid of enemies – fast!

Gypsy moth caterpillars

Gypsy moth caterpillars escape danger by dropping down on a line of silk and wafting away on the wind.

Stinkbugs

SEARCH & FIND
Can you find five small stinkbugs?
FIND & SEARCH

The weta is a huge insect, with long legs covered in spikes. When it's caught by a bird, the weta kicks with all its might, and is usually dropped in surprise!

Weta

A bombardier beetle fires at its enemies with a boiling hot stream of chemicals. It really stings!

Bombardier beetle

The screech beetle surprises its enemies with a loud squeak!

True or false?
You could read by the light of a glowworm.

Answer: **True**
Glowworms were once used as reading lamps. Their

glow lasts two hours or more.

I didn't know that

some bugs glow in the dark.

To find a mate, female fireflies make a light in their abdomen and flash signals to males. They are called glowworms.

When two ants meet, they often touch feelers in greeting.

Male staghorn beetles fight with each other for a female.

An insect's feelers aren't just for feeling. They help it to pick up smells in the air – and tastes and sounds, too.

SEARCH & FIND & SEARCH & FIND

Can you find the imposter?

A red mite is not an insect. It has eight legs.

When an ant finds some food, it marks the path to it with a strong-smelling scent. Other ants soon follow the scent and turn up to share the feast.

Five hundred years ago, rat fleas were the most dangerous insects in the world. They spread a deadly sickness called the plague, which killed millions and millions of people.

When the Queen Alexandra birdwing butterfly spreads its wings, it measures 11 inches (28 cm) from wingtip to wingtip. No wonder it's mistaken for a bird.

Fleas can jump an incredible 130 times their own height.

I didn't know that

a stick insect is the biggest insect in the world. The Indonesian giant stick insect measures more than 12 inches from head to toe. It's so big that it moves very slowly.

SEARCH & FIND SEARCH & FIND & SEARCH & FIND

Can you find ten fairy flies?

It's difficult to see real fairy flies – they are the size of a pin.

Male cicadas are the loudest insects in the world. Their clicking noise can be heard by females half a mile away.

Glossary

Abdomen
The last of the three parts of an insect's body.

Aphids
Tiny insects, such as greenflies, that feed by sucking up the juices from plants.

Beetles
A group of insects that has hard wingcases and can usually fly.

Camouflage
The colors and markings on an insect that help it to blend in with its surroundings, and make it difficult to see.

Caterpillar
The larva of a moth or butterfly.

Crickets
A group of insects that are related to grasshoppers and make a loud chirping noise.

Grub
The young caterpillarlike stage of a beetle and some other insects.

Larva (*plural*: larvae)
The young stage of an insect before metamorphosis. Caterpillars, maggots, and grubs are all types of larvae.

Metamorphosis
The change from the young stage to the adult stage of an insect. Many insects change from a larva, to a pupa, to a fully grown adult.

Nectar
The sweet liquid inside flowers, which attracts insects and other animals.

Nymph
The young stage of an insect that hatches looking just like its parents.

Pupa
The stage in an insect's life when it develops inside a hard, protective case.

Queen
The only egg-laying female in a nest of social insects, such as termites and bees.

Thorax
The middle part of an insect's body, between the head and the abdomen.

Wingcases
Hard outer wings that are not used for flying.

Index